B2B SAAS

For Beginners

The Comprehensive Guide To Learning How To Build A Successful Startup, How To Scale A Business, And How To Implement Pricing Models That Your Customers Will Love

B2B SAAS FOR BEGINNERS

The Comprehensive Guide To Learning How To Build A Successful Startup, How To Scale A Business, And How To Implement Pricing Models That Your Customers Will Love

While every precaution has been taken in the preparation of this book, the publisher assumes no responsibility for errors or omissions, or for damages resulting from the use of the information contained herein.

B2B SAAS FOR BEGINNERS: THE COMPREHENSIVE GUIDE TO LEARNING HOW TO BUILD A SUCCESSFUL STARTUP, HOW TO SCALE A BUSINESS, AND HOW TO IMPLEMENT PRICING MODELS THAT YOUR CUSTOMERS WILL LOVE

First Edition: August 26, 2024.

Written by Kid Montoya.

TABLE OF CONTENTS

CHAPTER 1

UNDERSTANDING B2B SAAS

Business-to-Business Software as a Service (B2B SaaS) refers to software solutions delivered via the cloud that cater specifically to the needs of businesses rather than individual consumers. Unlike traditional software, which requires physical installation and significant upfront costs, SaaS products are typically subscription-based and accessible online, allowing businesses to utilize sophisticated software without the need for extensive IT infrastructure.

Key Characteristics of B2B SaaS:

1. **Cloud-Based Delivery**: B2B SaaS products are hosted on remote servers and accessed through the internet, providing flexibility and ease of access from anywhere with an internet connection.

2. **Subscription Model**: Instead of a one-time purchase, customers pay a recurring fee, which could be monthly, annually, or based on usage. This model offers predictable revenue for providers and often reduces initial costs for users.

3. **Scalability**: B2B SaaS solutions are designed to scale with the business. As a company grows, it can easily upgrade its

subscription to accommodate more users or access additional features without significant overhauls.

4. **Multi-Tenancy**: Multiple customers (tenants) share the same software instance and infrastructure, with data isolated and secured for each tenant. This approach allows for efficient resource utilization and streamlined updates and maintenance.

5. **Automatic Updates and Maintenance**: The SaaS provider manages all updates, maintenance, and security patches, ensuring that clients always have access to the latest version without disruption or additional costs.

Benefits of B2B SaaS:

• **Cost-Effective**: Reduces the need for heavy upfront investments in software licenses, hardware, and IT personnel. Businesses can shift from a capital expenditure (CapEx) model to an operational expenditure (OpEx) model.

• **Flexibility and Accessibility**: Employees can access the software from anywhere, facilitating remote work and collaboration across different geographical locations.

• **Rapid Deployment**: B2B SaaS applications can be up and running much faster than traditional software, allowing businesses to realize value more quickly.

• **Continuous Improvement**: Providers regularly roll out new features and improvements based on user feedback and technological advancements, ensuring that the software evolves with the business needs.

Popular Use Cases for B2B SaaS:

- **Customer Relationship Management (CRM)**: Tools like Salesforce help businesses manage interactions with current and potential customers, streamline processes, and improve profitability.

- **Enterprise Resource Planning (ERP)**: Solutions like SAP S/4HANA and Oracle ERP Cloud integrate core business processes, providing real-time data and analytics to improve decision-making.

- **Human Resources Management (HRM)**: Platforms such as Workday and BambooHR assist in managing employee data, payroll, recruitment, and performance.

- **Project Management**: Tools like Asana, Trello, and Jira help teams plan, track, and manage projects efficiently, enhancing productivity and collaboration.

- **Marketing Automation**: Solutions like HubSpot and Marketo automate marketing tasks, from email campaigns to lead generation, helping businesses attract and retain customers.

B2B SaaS Market Trends:

- **AI and Machine Learning**: Increasingly integrated into SaaS products to provide advanced analytics, automation, and personalized user experiences.

- **Vertical SaaS**: Tailored solutions for specific industries (e.g., healthcare, finance, legal) offering specialized features and compliance capabilities.

- **Enhanced Security**: With growing concerns over data breaches, SaaS providers are investing heavily in robust security measures to protect sensitive business data.

B2B SaaS has revolutionized how businesses operate by providing scalable, cost-effective, and efficient software solutions that drive growth and innovation. As technology continues to advance, the B2B SaaS landscape will likely evolve, offering even more sophisticated tools to meet the dynamic needs of businesses.

- **Key Differences Between B2B and B2C SaaS**

B2B SaaS (Business-to-Business Software as a Service) and **B2C SaaS (Business-to-Consumer Software as a Service)** serve distinct markets, and while both models deliver software over the internet, their target audiences, sales processes, product features, and customer expectations differ significantly. Understanding these differences is crucial for developing effective strategies tailored to each market.

1. Target Audience

- **B2B SaaS**: Targets businesses and organizations. The users are typically professionals seeking solutions that enhance productivity, streamline operations, or provide specific business functionalities.

- **B2C SaaS**: Targets individual consumers. The users are general consumers looking for personal use software, entertainment, social connectivity, or lifestyle enhancements.

2. Sales and Marketing Approach

- **B2B SaaS**: Sales cycles are often longer and more complex, involving multiple decision-makers and stakeholders. Marketing efforts focus on demonstrating ROI, efficiency improvements, and solving specific business problems. Techniques include account-based marketing, detailed demos, whitepapers, and case studies.

- **B2C SaaS**: Sales cycles are typically shorter and more straightforward, often driven by impulse purchases or immediate needs. Marketing efforts focus on broad appeal, user experience, and emotional engagement. Techniques include social media campaigns, influencer marketing, freemium models, and user reviews.

3. Pricing Models

- **B2B SaaS**: Pricing is usually higher and more complex, often based on the number of users, usage volume, or specific features required. Custom pricing and enterprise deals are common, with options for annual or multi-year contracts.

- **B2C SaaS**: Pricing is usually lower and simpler, often involving one-time payments, monthly or annual subscriptions, and freemium models with in-app purchases or ads.

4. Customer Onboarding and Support

- **B2B SaaS**: Onboarding processes are comprehensive, often involving personalized training, dedicated support teams, and extensive documentation. Ongoing customer support and success programs are crucial for retention.

- **B2C SaaS**: Onboarding is generally self-service and intuitive, with minimal setup required. Support is typically provided through FAQs, chatbots, and community forums.

5. Product Features and Customization

- **B2B SaaS**: Products are feature-rich, customizable, and designed to integrate with existing business systems. They often include advanced analytics, security features, compliance tools, and scalability options to accommodate business growth.

- **B2C SaaS**: Products focus on user experience, simplicity, and ease of use. Features are designed for mass appeal and immediate gratification, with less emphasis on customization and integration.

6. Renewal and Retention Strategies

- **B2B SaaS**: Renewal strategies involve personalized outreach, performance reviews, and demonstrating continued value. Retention efforts focus on building strong relationships through dedicated account managers and proactive customer success initiatives.

- **B2C SaaS**: Renewal strategies rely on automated reminders, special offers, and easy renewal processes. Retention efforts focus on user engagement through regular updates, new features, and community building.

7. Metrics and KPIs

- **B2B SaaS**: Key metrics include customer acquisition cost (CAC), customer lifetime value (CLV), monthly recurring revenue (MRR), churn rate, and net promoter score (NPS). Detailed tracking of user behavior, feature adoption, and usage patterns is essential.

- **B2C SaaS**: Key metrics include daily active users (DAU), monthly active users (MAU), churn rate, conversion rates from freemium to paid plans, and customer satisfaction ratings. Emphasis is placed on user engagement and growth metrics.

8. Sales Channels

- **B2B SaaS**: Sales often involve direct channels, including field sales, inside sales, and channel partners. Relationships and reputation play a significant role in the buying process.

- **B2C SaaS**: Sales are primarily through digital channels, such as app stores, websites, and online advertisements. The process is largely self-service, driven by marketing efforts and user reviews.

Understanding these key differences helps businesses tailor their strategies to meet the unique needs and expectations of their target markets, whether they're aiming to serve other businesses or individual consumers.

- **Common Myths and Misconceptions About B2B SaaS**

The world of B2B SaaS is rife with myths and misconceptions that can mislead potential entrepreneurs, investors, and even users. Dispelling these myths is essential for a clear understanding of the opportunities and challenges within the B2B SaaS landscape.

Myth 1: B2B SaaS is Only for Large Enterprises

- **Reality**: While many large enterprises utilize B2B SaaS solutions, these products are also designed for small and medium-sized businesses (SMBs). SaaS models offer scalable solutions that can grow with a business, making them accessible and valuable to companies of all sizes.

Myth 2: B2B SaaS is Just Like B2C SaaS

- **Reality**: Although both models involve delivering software via the cloud, B2B and B2C SaaS cater to fundamentally different audiences with distinct needs. B2B SaaS focuses on solving specific business problems, often requiring complex features, customization, and integration capabilities. B2C SaaS prioritizes user experience and simplicity for individual consumers.

Myth 3: SaaS Products are Inherently Secure

- **Reality**: While SaaS providers invest heavily in security measures, the responsibility for data security is shared between the provider and the customer. Businesses must ensure they follow best practices in data protection, access control, and compliance with industry standards to safeguard their information.

Myth 4: B2B SaaS Solutions are Expensive

- **Reality**: B2B SaaS solutions can be cost-effective, particularly when considering the total cost of ownership (TCO) compared to traditional software. SaaS eliminates the need for significant upfront investments in hardware and licenses, offering predictable subscription costs and reducing the burden on in-house IT resources.

Myth 5: Once Deployed, SaaS Runs Itself

- **Reality**: Successful B2B SaaS implementation requires ongoing management, including regular updates, user training, and support. Continuous engagement with the SaaS provider ensures that the business leverages the latest features and maintains optimal performance.

Myth 6: SaaS Can't Handle Mission-Critical Applications

- **Reality**: Many B2B SaaS solutions are designed to support mission-critical applications with high availability, reliability, and security. Providers offer robust service level agreements (SLAs) and disaster recovery plans to ensure business continuity.

Myth 7: Customization is Limited in SaaS

- **Reality**: While early SaaS offerings were often rigid, modern B2B SaaS solutions provide extensive customization options. APIs, configurable workflows, and modular architectures allow businesses to tailor the software to their specific needs without compromising on scalability.

Myth 8: SaaS is Only for Tech-Savvy Businesses

- **Reality**: SaaS solutions are designed to be user-friendly and accessible to businesses across various industries, regardless of their technical expertise. Providers often offer comprehensive support, training resources, and intuitive interfaces to ensure ease of use.

Myth 9: SaaS Adoption Leads to Job Losses in IT

- **Reality**: Rather than eliminating IT jobs, SaaS can transform them. IT teams can shift their focus from routine maintenance and infrastructure management to strategic initiatives, innovation, and value-added activities that drive business growth.

Myth 10: SaaS is a Passing Trend

- **Reality**: SaaS has firmly established itself as a dominant model in the software industry, with continuous growth and innovation. Its benefits in terms of cost, scalability, and flexibility ensure its relevance and adoption for years to come.

By debunking these myths, businesses can make informed decisions about adopting and implementing B2B SaaS solutions, leveraging their full potential to drive efficiency, innovation, and growth.

- **Case Studies of Successful B2B SaaS Companies**

1. Salesforce

Overview: Salesforce, founded in 1999 by Marc Benioff, is a pioneer in the B2B SaaS industry, offering a comprehensive Customer Relationship Management (CRM) platform. Its cloud-based solutions help businesses manage customer interactions, sales, and marketing.

Challenges:

- Breaking into an established market dominated by on-premise software.

- Convincing businesses to trust cloud-based solutions with their sensitive customer data.

Solutions:

- Salesforce focused on creating a user-friendly, scalable, and secure CRM platform.

- They offered a subscription-based model, reducing upfront costs for businesses.

- Invested heavily in marketing and educating potential customers about the benefits of SaaS and cloud computing.

Results:

- Salesforce revolutionized the CRM industry and became a market leader.

- It expanded its offerings to include various cloud services, such as analytics, marketing automation, and application development.

- The company achieved a market capitalization of over $200 billion, serving millions of users worldwide.

2. Slack

Overview: Slack, founded in 2013 by Stewart Butterfield, provides a messaging platform designed for team collaboration. It simplifies communication and integrates with numerous third-party services.

Challenges:

- Entering a crowded market with established competitors like Microsoft Teams and HipChat.

- Convincing businesses to adopt a new communication tool.

Solutions:

- Slack focused on creating a highly intuitive and user-friendly interface.

- They emphasized integration capabilities, allowing users to connect Slack with various tools they already used.

- Employed a freemium model, enabling teams to try the product before committing to a paid plan.

Results:

- Slack quickly gained popularity, becoming a staple in modern workplaces.

- Acquired by Salesforce in 2021 for $27.7 billion, further expanding its reach and capabilities.

- Continues to innovate and add features, maintaining a strong presence in the market.

3. HubSpot

12

Overview: HubSpot, founded in 2006 by Brian Halligan and Dharmesh Shah, offers an inbound marketing, sales, and service platform. It helps businesses attract visitors, convert leads, and close customers.

Challenges:

• Competing against well-established marketing automation tools.

• Educating businesses on the benefits of inbound marketing.

Solutions:

• HubSpot developed an all-in-one platform with tools for content management, social media marketing, lead generation, and customer relationship management.

• They pioneered the concept of inbound marketing, focusing on creating valuable content to attract and engage customers.

• Offered extensive educational resources, including blogs, webinars, and certifications, to help businesses understand and implement inbound marketing strategies.

Results:

• HubSpot grew rapidly, becoming a leader in the marketing automation space.

• Went public in 2014 and continues to expand its product offerings and customer base.

• Serves over 100,000 customers in more than 120 countries.

4. Zoom

Overview: Zoom, founded in 2011 by Eric Yuan, provides a cloud-based video conferencing service. It enables seamless communication through video, voice, and chat across various devices.

Challenges:

• Competing with established players like Skype, WebEx, and Google Hangouts.

• Ensuring reliable and high-quality video and audio performance.

Solutions:

• Zoom focused on delivering a superior user experience with high-quality video and audio.

• They emphasized ease of use, scalability, and integration with existing workflows.

• Adopted a freemium model, allowing users to try the platform before upgrading to paid plans.

Results:

• Zoom experienced explosive growth, particularly during the COVID-19 pandemic.

• Became synonymous with video conferencing, expanding its user base to millions worldwide.

- Achieved a market capitalization of over $100 billion and continues to innovate with new features and services.

5. ServiceNow

Overview: ServiceNow, founded in 2004 by Fred Luddy, offers a cloud-based platform for IT service management (ITSM). It helps organizations automate and streamline their IT operations.

Challenges:

- Entering a market dominated by traditional ITSM solutions.

- Convincing businesses to move their IT operations to the cloud.

Solutions:

- ServiceNow developed a robust, scalable, and flexible ITSM platform.

- They focused on automation and integration capabilities, enabling businesses to improve efficiency and reduce costs.

- Offered a comprehensive suite of IT operations management (ITOM) and IT business management (ITBM) tools.

Results:

- ServiceNow quickly gained traction, becoming a leader in the ITSM market.

- Expanded its offerings to include HR, customer service, and other enterprise service management solutions.

- Achieved a market capitalization of over $100 billion, serving thousands of customers globally.

These case studies illustrate how B2B SaaS companies have successfully navigated challenges, leveraged innovative solutions, and achieved remarkable growth. They highlight the potential of B2B SaaS to transform industries and drive business success.

CHAPTER 2
BUILDING YOUR B2B SAAS STARTUP

Identifying a market need and validating your idea is the critical first step in building a successful B2B SaaS startup. It ensures that your product solves a real problem for your target audience and has the potential for market acceptance and growth.

1. Conduct Market Research

- **Industry Analysis**: Study the industry you plan to enter. Identify trends, challenges, and opportunities. Resources like industry reports, market analysis studies, and news articles can provide valuable insights.

- **Competitor Analysis**: Identify existing competitors and analyze their strengths, weaknesses, opportunities, and threats (SWOT analysis). Understand their product offerings, pricing models, and customer feedback.

- **Customer Interviews**: Speak directly with potential customers to understand their pain points, needs, and preferences. Use surveys, focus groups, and one-on-one interviews to gather qualitative data.

2. Define Your Target Market

- **Segmentation**: Break down the broader market into smaller, more manageable segments based on factors like company size, industry, geographic location, and specific needs.

- **Buyer Personas**: Create detailed profiles of your ideal customers, including their demographics, job roles, challenges, and goals. This helps tailor your product and marketing strategies to meet their needs.

3. Identify Pain Points

- **Problem Identification**: Determine the specific problems your target market is facing. These could be inefficiencies in their processes, gaps in existing solutions, or emerging challenges due to market changes.

- **Solution Fit**: Ensure that your product idea directly addresses these pain points. It should offer a solution that is significantly better, faster, or cheaper than existing alternatives.

4. Validate Your Idea

- **Minimum Viable Product (MVP)**: Develop an MVP to test your idea with real users. The MVP should include core features that solve the main pain points of your target market.

- **Pilot Programs**: Launch pilot programs with a small group of users to gather feedback and iterate on your product. This helps refine your solution based on real-world usage.

- **Metrics and Feedback**: Track key metrics such as user engagement, retention rates, and satisfaction levels. Collect qualitative feedback to understand what users like and dislike about your product.

5. Adjust and Pivot if Necessary

- **Iterative Development**: Use feedback and data from your MVP and pilot programs to make necessary adjustments to your product. This iterative process ensures that you are continuously improving and aligning with market needs.

- **Pivoting**: Be prepared to pivot your idea if initial validation indicates that the market need is different from what you anticipated. Pivoting can involve changing your target market, altering your product features, or even exploring new business models.

6. Build a Value Proposition

- **Unique Selling Proposition (USP)**: Clearly define what sets your product apart from competitors. Your USP should highlight the unique benefits and value your product offers.

- **Customer Benefits**: Focus on the tangible benefits your customers will experience by using your product, such as increased efficiency, cost savings, or improved performance.

7. Competitive Advantage

- **Sustainable Advantage**: Identify factors that will give your product a sustainable competitive advantage, such as proprietary technology, superior customer service, or exclusive partnerships.

Crafting Your Business Plan and Vision

A well-crafted business plan and vision provide a roadmap for your B2B SaaS startup, guiding your strategic decisions and attracting potential investors and stakeholders.

1. Executive Summary

- **Overview**: Provide a concise overview of your business, including your mission statement, product offering, target market, and key objectives.

- **Vision and Mission**: Clearly articulate your long-term vision and mission. The vision should describe the future impact you aim to achieve, while the mission should explain how you intend to achieve it.

2. Company Description

- **Business Structure**: Detail your company's legal structure (e.g., LLC, corporation) and ownership.

- **Company History**: Include relevant background information, such as the founders' experience and the origin of the business idea.

3. Market Analysis

- **Industry Overview**: Summarize the industry landscape, including market size, growth trends, and key drivers.

- **Target Market**: Define your target market segments and buyer personas in detail. Highlight the specific needs and pain points you aim to address.

4. Product Description

- **Core Features**: Describe your product's core features and how they address the identified market needs.

- **Unique Selling Proposition (USP)**: Explain what differentiates your product from competitors and why customers should choose it.

5. Marketing and Sales Strategy

- **Go-to-Market Plan**: Outline your strategy for launching and promoting your product. Include details on marketing channels, messaging, and campaigns.

- **Sales Strategy**: Describe your sales approach, including the sales funnel, lead generation tactics, and customer acquisition strategies.

6. Business Model and Revenue Streams

- **Pricing Strategy**: Define your pricing model, whether it's subscription-based, tiered, usage-based, or another structure. Explain how your pricing aligns with market expectations and competitor offerings.

- **Revenue Projections**: Provide detailed revenue projections, including assumptions and key drivers. Include scenarios for best-case, worst-case, and most likely outcomes.

7. Operations Plan

- **Product Development**: Describe your product development process, including timelines, milestones, and key deliverables.

- **Operational Structure**: Outline your operational structure, including key departments, roles, and responsibilities.

8. Financial Plan

- **Funding Requirements**: Detail your funding requirements, including how much capital you need, what it will be used for, and your funding strategy (e.g., venture capital, angel investors, bootstrapping).

- **Financial Projections**: Provide financial projections for the next three to five years, including income statements, cash flow statements, and balance sheets.

- **Break-Even Analysis**: Include a break-even analysis to show when your business is expected to become profitable.

9. Risk Analysis and Mitigation

- **Identify Risks**: Identify potential risks and challenges your business might face, such as market competition, regulatory changes, or technological advancements.

- **Mitigation Strategies**: Outline strategies to mitigate these risks and ensure business continuity.

10. Appendix

- **Supporting Documents**: Include any additional supporting documents, such as resumes of key team members, market research data, product prototypes, and legal agreements.

Crafting a thorough business plan and a compelling vision sets a solid foundation for your B2B SaaS startup, providing direction and clarity as you navigate the journey of building, scaling, and sustaining your business.

- **Assembling Your Founding Team: Roles and Responsibilities**

Building a successful B2B SaaS startup requires a strong founding team with complementary skills and a shared vision. Here are the key roles and responsibilities typically needed for a B2B SaaS company:

1. Chief Executive Officer (CEO)

- **Responsibilities**: Provides overall strategic direction, oversees company operations, and represents the company to investors, customers, and partners. The CEO ensures the company stays on track to meet its long-term goals.

- **Skills**: Leadership, strategic thinking, communication, and business acumen.

2. Chief Technology Officer (CTO)

- **Responsibilities**: Oversees the development and implementation of the technology strategy. The CTO is responsible for the product's architecture, technology stack, and ensuring the product is scalable and secure.

- **Skills**: Software development, systems architecture, technical leadership, and innovation.

3. Chief Product Officer (CPO)

- **Responsibilities**: Manages the product vision, strategy, and roadmap. The CPO ensures that the product meets market needs, oversees product development, and manages the product lifecycle.

- **Skills**: Product management, market research, user experience (UX) design, and strategic planning.

4. Chief Marketing Officer (CMO)

- **Responsibilities**: Develops and executes the marketing strategy to build brand awareness, generate leads, and drive customer acquisition. The CMO oversees marketing campaigns, content creation, and public relations.

- **Skills**: Marketing strategy, digital marketing, content creation, and analytics.

5. Chief Sales Officer (CSO)

- **Responsibilities**: Leads the sales strategy and manages the sales team. The CSO is responsible for developing sales processes, setting targets, and building relationships with key customers.

- **Skills**: Sales strategy, relationship management, negotiation, and leadership.

6. Chief Financial Officer (CFO)

- **Responsibilities**: Manages the company's financial health, including budgeting, forecasting, and financial reporting. The CFO oversees funding strategies, investor relations, and ensures financial compliance.

- **Skills**: Financial planning, accounting, risk management, and strategic analysis.

7. Head of Customer Success

- **Responsibilities**: Ensures customers are satisfied and achieve their desired outcomes with the product. The Head of Customer Success manages onboarding, support, and retention strategies.

- **Skills**: Customer relationship management, problem-solving, communication, and empathy.

Initial Funding Options and Financial Planning

Securing initial funding and having a robust financial plan are critical for the launch and growth of a B2B SaaS startup. Here are the common funding options and key aspects of financial planning:

1. Funding Options

- **Bootstrapping**: Using personal savings and revenue generated from the business to fund operations. This approach avoids debt and equity dilution but may limit growth potential.

- **Friends and Family**: Raising funds from personal connections who believe in your vision. This can be a quick way to secure initial capital but involves personal risk.

- **Angel Investors**: Securing investment from high-net-worth individuals who provide capital in exchange for equity. Angel investors often bring valuable industry experience and connections.

- **Venture Capital (VC)**: Raising significant capital from venture capital firms that specialize in high-growth startups. VCs provide large amounts of funding and strategic support but require equity and influence in company decisions.

- **Crowdfunding**: Using platforms like Kickstarter or Indiegogo to raise small amounts of money from a large number of people. This can validate your idea and build a community around your product.

- **Grants and Competitions**: Applying for government grants, startup competitions, or incubator programs that provide non-dilutive funding and resources.

2. Financial Planning

- **Budgeting**: Create a detailed budget that outlines your expected revenues, expenses, and capital requirements. Include costs for product development, marketing, sales, operations, and salaries.

- **Cash Flow Management**: Monitor your cash flow to ensure you have sufficient liquidity to meet your obligations. Plan for contingencies and avoid overextending your finances.

- **Revenue Projections**: Develop realistic revenue projections based on market research, sales forecasts, and pricing strategies. Include different scenarios (best-case, worst-case, and most likely).

- **Expense Management**: Track and control your expenses to avoid unnecessary costs. Regularly review your financial statements and make adjustments as needed.

- **Break-Even Analysis**: Calculate your break-even point to understand when your business will become profitable. This helps in setting financial goals and making informed decisions.

Creating a Minimum Viable Product (MVP)

A Minimum Viable Product (MVP) is a version of your product with the minimum features necessary to solve the core problem and validate your idea with early users. The MVP allows you to gather feedback, iterate, and develop a product that meets market needs.

1. Define Core Features

- **Identify the Problem**: Clearly define the problem your product aims to solve. Focus on the most critical pain points of your target market.

- **Prioritize Features**: List all potential features and prioritize them based on their importance to solving the core problem. Include only the essential features in your MVP.

2. Develop the MVP

- **Design**: Create a simple, user-friendly design that allows users to interact with the core features of your product. Ensure the design is intuitive and easy to navigate.

- **Build**: Develop the MVP using agile methodologies to ensure quick iterations and improvements. Focus on functionality and reliability over aesthetics.

- **Test**: Conduct thorough testing to identify and fix any bugs or issues. Ensure the MVP performs well under real-world conditions.

3. Launch and Gather Feedback

- **Launch to Early Adopters**: Release the MVP to a select group of early adopters who are representative of your target market. Use beta testing programs or invite-only access to manage the rollout.

- **Collect Feedback**: Gather feedback from users through surveys, interviews, and usage analytics. Understand what works well and what needs improvement.

- **Analyze Data**: Analyze the feedback and usage data to identify patterns, pain points, and areas for enhancement. Use this information to prioritize future development.

4. Iterate and Improve

- **Refine Features**: Based on user feedback, refine existing features and add new ones that enhance the product's value.

- **Enhance User Experience**: Improve the user interface and experience to ensure the product is engaging and easy to use.

- **Scale Gradually**: As the product matures, gradually scale it by adding more features, expanding your user base, and improving infrastructure.

5. Validate Market Fit

- **Measure Success**: Use key performance indicators (KPIs) such as user engagement, retention rates, and customer satisfaction to measure the success of your MVP.

- **Adjust Strategy**: Be prepared to pivot or adjust your strategy based on the feedback and data you collect. Continuous improvement is essential for achieving product-market fit.

By assembling a strong founding team, securing initial funding, and creating a well-defined MVP, you set the foundation for a successful B2B SaaS startup. Each step builds upon the previous one, ensuring that your product is aligned with market needs and poised for growth.

CHAPTER 3

DEVELOPING YOUR SAAS PRODUCT

The product development lifecycle in a B2B SaaS startup encompasses the stages from initial concept to product launch and beyond. Each phase is crucial for creating a product that meets market needs and achieves business objectives.

1. Ideation

- **Problem Identification**: Identify a market need or problem that your product aims to solve.

- **Brainstorming**: Generate ideas and solutions. Involve stakeholders, including potential customers, to gather diverse perspectives.

- **Feasibility Analysis**: Assess the technical, financial, and market feasibility of your ideas.

2. Market Research and Validation

- **Target Market**: Define your target audience and create detailed buyer personas.

- **Competitor Analysis**: Study existing solutions to understand the competitive landscape.

- **Validation**: Use surveys, interviews, and MVP testing to validate your idea with real users.

3. Planning

- **Roadmap**: Develop a product roadmap outlining key milestones, features, and timelines.

- **Requirements**: Gather and document functional and non-functional requirements.

- **Budget and Resources**: Estimate the budget and resources needed for development.

4. Design

- **User Experience (UX)**: Create user personas and user journey maps to ensure a seamless experience.

- **Wireframes and Prototypes**: Design wireframes and interactive prototypes to visualize the product.

- **User Interface (UI)**: Develop a visually appealing and intuitive user interface.

5. Development

- **Tech Stack Selection**: Choose the appropriate technologies, frameworks, and tools for your product.

- **Agile Methodology**: Implement agile development practices for iterative progress and continuous improvement.

- **Coding and Integration**: Develop the product, focusing on core features first. Integrate third-party services as needed.

6. Testing

- **Unit Testing**: Test individual components to ensure they function correctly.

- **Integration Testing**: Verify that different modules work together as expected.

- **User Acceptance Testing (UAT)**: Involve end-users in testing to ensure the product meets their needs.

- **Performance Testing**: Assess the product's performance under various conditions.

7. Deployment

- **Staging Environment**: Deploy the product in a staging environment for final testing.

- **Production Environment**: Deploy the product to the live environment, ensuring minimal downtime.

- **Monitoring**: Set up monitoring tools to track performance and user activity.

8. Launch

- **Marketing Plan**: Execute a marketing plan to promote the product launch.

- **Customer Support**: Provide customer support to address any issues users may encounter.

- **Feedback Loop**: Collect feedback from users to identify areas for improvement.

9. Maintenance and Iteration

- **Bug Fixes**: Address any bugs or issues that arise post-launch.

- **Feature Enhancements**: Continuously improve the product based on user feedback and market trends.

- **Scalability**: Ensure the product can scale to accommodate growing user numbers and demands.

Choosing the Right Tech Stack for Your SaaS Product

Selecting the right tech stack is essential for building a scalable, secure, and maintainable SaaS product. The tech stack includes the programming languages, frameworks, libraries, and tools used in development.

1. Front-End Development

- **Languages**: HTML, CSS, JavaScript.

- **Frameworks/Libraries**: React, Angular, Vue.js.

- **Considerations**: Choose a framework that ensures a responsive and dynamic user interface. React is popular for its flexibility and component-based architecture.

2. Back-End Development

- **Languages**: JavaScript (Node.js), Python, Ruby, Java, PHP.

- **Frameworks**: Express.js (Node.js), Django (Python), Ruby on Rails, Spring (Java), Laravel (PHP).

- **Considerations**: Select a language and framework that support scalability, maintainability, and performance. Node.js with Express.js is a popular choice for its asynchronous capabilities and large ecosystem.

3. Database

- **Relational Databases**: MySQL, PostgreSQL.

- **NoSQL Databases**: MongoDB, Cassandra.

- **Considerations**: Choose a database that aligns with your data structure and scalability needs. PostgreSQL is favored for its robustness and support for complex queries.

4. Cloud Infrastructure

- **Providers**: AWS, Google Cloud Platform (GCP), Microsoft Azure.

- **Services**: Compute (EC2, GCE), Storage (S3, Google Cloud Storage), Databases (RDS, Cloud SQL), Serverless (Lambda, Cloud Functions).

- **Considerations**: Opt for a provider that offers comprehensive services, scalability, and global reach. AWS is widely used for its extensive services and reliability.

5. DevOps and CI/CD

- **Tools**: Docker, Kubernetes, Jenkins, Travis CI, CircleCI.

- **Considerations**: Implement containerization and orchestration for scalability and consistency. Use CI/CD tools to automate testing and deployment processes.

6. Security

- **Practices**: Implement security best practices, including encryption, secure authentication, and regular vulnerability assessments.

- **Tools**: Use tools like OWASP ZAP for security testing and monitoring.

7. Monitoring and Analytics

- **Tools**: New Relic, Datadog, Google Analytics, Mixpanel.

- **Considerations**: Set up monitoring and analytics to track performance, user behavior, and application health.

8. API Development

- **Tools**: Postman, Swagger, GraphQL.

- **Considerations**: Use tools that facilitate API design, documentation, and testing. Swagger is popular for RESTful APIs, while GraphQL offers a flexible query language.

9. Version Control

- **Tools**: Git, GitHub, GitLab, Bitbucket.

- **Considerations**: Use version control systems to manage code changes and collaboration effectively. GitHub is widely used for its integration capabilities and community support.

Choosing the right tech stack involves balancing performance, scalability, security, and ease of development. It should align with your product requirements and your team's expertise, ensuring a strong foundation for your SaaS product.

- **Ensuring Scalability and Security from the Start**

Ensuring scalability and security from the beginning is crucial for the success of a B2B SaaS product. Scalability ensures that your product can handle growing user demands, while security protects sensitive data and maintains user trust.

1. Scalability

- **Architecture Design**: Design your system architecture to be modular and distributed. Use microservices or serverless architectures to manage different components independently and scale them as needed.

- **Load Balancing**: Implement load balancing to distribute incoming traffic evenly across multiple servers. This helps prevent any single server from becoming a bottleneck.

- **Database Scaling**: Choose a database that supports horizontal scaling (sharding) and can handle increased data loads. For NoSQL databases, ensure they support partitioning and replication.

- **Caching**: Use caching mechanisms to reduce database load and improve response times. Tools like Redis or Memcached can cache frequently accessed data.

- **Auto-Scaling**: Configure auto-scaling for your compute resources to automatically adjust capacity based on traffic or load. Cloud providers like AWS, GCP, and Azure offer auto-scaling services.

- **Performance Monitoring**: Implement performance monitoring and alerting to detect and address issues proactively. Use tools like New Relic or Datadog to monitor application performance and server health.

2. Security

- **Data Encryption**: Encrypt data at rest and in transit using robust encryption standards (e.g., AES-256 for data at rest and TLS for data in transit). This protects sensitive information from unauthorized access.

- **Authentication and Authorization**: Implement strong authentication mechanisms, such as multi-factor authentication (MFA), to verify user identities. Use role-based access control (RBAC) to manage user permissions and prevent unauthorized access.

- **Vulnerability Management**: Regularly update and patch software to fix security vulnerabilities. Conduct vulnerability assessments and penetration testing to identify and address potential weaknesses.

- **Secure Coding Practices**: Follow secure coding practices to prevent common security issues such as SQL injection, cross-site scripting (XSS), and cross-site request forgery (CSRF).

- **Regular Audits and Compliance**: Perform regular security audits and ensure compliance with relevant regulations and standards (e.g., GDPR, HIPAA). Keep up-to-date with best practices and industry standards.

- **Incident Response Plan**: Develop and maintain an incident response plan to handle security breaches effectively. This should include procedures for identifying, containing, and mitigating incidents.

User Experience and User Interface Design Best Practices

Creating an excellent user experience (UX) and user interface (UI) is essential for the success of your B2B SaaS product. Good design improves usability, engagement, and satisfaction.

1. User Experience (UX)

- **Understand User Needs**: Conduct user research to understand the needs, goals, and pain points of your target audience. Use methods like surveys, interviews, and user testing.

- **User Personas**: Create detailed user personas to guide design decisions. Personas should represent different segments of your target audience and their specific needs.

- **Clear Navigation**: Design intuitive navigation to help users find information and complete tasks easily. Use clear labels, consistent layouts, and logical flow.

- **Usability Testing**: Conduct usability testing to identify and address issues with the user experience. Observe real users interacting with your product and gather feedback.

- **Accessibility**: Ensure your product is accessible to users with disabilities. Follow accessibility guidelines (e.g., WCAG) and use semantic HTML, keyboard navigation, and screen reader support.

- **Feedback Mechanisms**: Implement feedback mechanisms such as surveys, in-app feedback forms, or support channels to gather user input and continuously improve the experience.

2. User Interface (UI)

- **Consistency**: Maintain visual consistency across your product to create a cohesive experience. Use consistent colors, fonts, and design elements throughout.

- **Visual Hierarchy**: Establish a clear visual hierarchy to guide users' attention to important elements. Use size, color, and placement to differentiate between primary and secondary actions.

- **Responsiveness**: Design a responsive interface that adapts to different screen sizes and devices. Ensure that your product works well on desktops, tablets, and smartphones.

- **Performance**: Optimize UI elements to ensure fast loading times and smooth interactions. Minimize the use of heavy images and scripts that can slow down the user experience.

- **Microinteractions**: Incorporate microinteractions (e.g., animations, hover effects) to enhance user engagement and provide visual feedback on actions.

- **Onboarding**: Provide an effective onboarding process to help new users get started with your product. Use guided tours, tooltips, and tutorials to explain key features and functionalities.

Iterative Development and Agile Methodologies

Iterative development and agile methodologies enable flexible and adaptive product development. They help teams respond to changes and deliver value incrementally.

1. Agile Methodologies

- **Scrum**: Scrum is an agile framework that uses time-boxed iterations called sprints (usually 2-4 weeks) to develop and deliver product increments. Teams hold regular ceremonies such as sprint planning, daily stand-ups, and sprint reviews to manage progress and adapt to changes.

- **Kanban**: Kanban focuses on visualizing work and optimizing workflow. Teams use Kanban boards to manage tasks, track progress, and identify bottlenecks. Kanban emphasizes continuous delivery and improvement.

- **Extreme Programming (XP)**: XP emphasizes technical excellence and customer collaboration. It includes practices like pair programming, test-driven development (TDD), and continuous integration to improve code quality and responsiveness.

2. Iterative Development

- **Incremental Releases**: Develop and release small, functional increments of your product. Each increment adds value and allows users to provide feedback on new features or improvements.

- **Feedback Loop**: Use feedback from users and stakeholders to inform the development of subsequent iterations. Iterate based on real-world usage and changing requirements.

- **Continuous Improvement**: Regularly review and refine processes, practices, and features to enhance the product and development efficiency. Hold retrospectives to identify areas for improvement and implement changes.

- **Prototyping**: Create prototypes to test ideas and validate concepts before full-scale development. Prototypes can be low-fidelity (e.g., sketches) or high-fidelity (e.g., interactive mockups) and help in gathering early feedback.

3. Collaboration and Communication

- **Cross-Functional Teams**: Assemble cross-functional teams with diverse skills (e.g., developers, designers, product managers) to ensure comprehensive development and faster decision-making.

- **Transparent Communication**: Foster open and transparent communication among team members. Use collaboration tools like Slack, Microsoft Teams, or Jira to facilitate information sharing and coordination.

By focusing on scalability, security, UX/UI design, and adopting iterative and agile methodologies, you can build a robust and user-centered B2B SaaS product that meets market demands and adapts to evolving needs.

CHAPTER 4
GO-TO-MARKET STRATEGY

Understanding your target market and creating detailed customer personas are foundational steps in building a successful B2B SaaS product. This process helps ensure that your product meets the needs and preferences of your ideal customers.

1. Target Market Analysis

- **Market Research**: Conduct thorough market research to identify and analyze your target market. Use methods like surveys, interviews, and industry reports to gather data on market size, trends, and customer needs.

- **Segmentation**: Divide your target market into distinct segments based on factors such as industry, company size, geographic location, and job roles. This helps tailor your product and marketing efforts to specific groups.

- **Competitor Analysis**: Analyze your competitors to understand their offerings, strengths, and weaknesses. Identify gaps in the market that your product can fill or areas where you can differentiate yourself.

- **Market Needs and Pain Points**: Identify the key challenges and pain points faced by your target market. Understand what solutions they currently use and what improvements they seek.

2. Customer Personas

- **Creating Personas**: Develop detailed customer personas that represent your ideal customers. Each persona should include demographic information, job roles, goals, challenges, and behaviors.

  - o   **Demographics**: Include age, gender, education, and other relevant demographic details.

  - o   **Job Role**: Specify the job title, responsibilities, and decision-making authority of the persona.

  - o   **Goals and Objectives**: Outline the goals and objectives that the persona aims to achieve in their role.

  - o   **Challenges and Pain Points**: Identify the challenges and pain points that the persona encounters and how your product can address them.

  - o   **Behavior and Preferences**: Describe the persona's preferences, such as preferred communication channels, purchasing behaviors, and technology usage.

- **Persona Scenarios**: Create scenarios or use cases that demonstrate how each persona interacts with your product. This helps in understanding their needs and designing solutions that fit their context.

- **Validating Personas**: Validate your personas through interviews, surveys, and user feedback. Ensure that they accurately represent your target audience and adjust them based on real-world data.

- **Utilizing Personas**: Use your customer personas to guide product development, marketing strategies, and sales efforts. Tailor your messaging, features, and user experience to align with the needs and preferences of each persona.

Building a Strong Brand Identity

A strong brand identity helps differentiate your B2B SaaS product in a competitive market, fosters trust, and creates a lasting impression with customers.

1. Brand Positioning

- **Unique Value Proposition (UVP)**: Define your unique value proposition that clearly communicates the benefits and value of your product. Focus on what sets your product apart from competitors and how it solves customer problems.

- **Brand Promise**: Articulate the promise your brand makes to customers. This should align with your UVP and convey the core benefits and experiences customers can expect.

2. Brand Elements

- **Brand Name**: Choose a brand name that is memorable, relevant, and easy to pronounce. Ensure it resonates with your target audience and reflects your brand values.

- **Logo**: Design a distinctive and visually appealing logo that represents your brand. The logo should be versatile and work well across different media and sizes.

- **Color Palette**: Develop a color palette that reflects your brand personality and appeals to your target audience. Use colors consistently across all brand materials to create a cohesive look.

- **Typography**: Select fonts that align with your brand's tone and style. Use typography consistently in all communications to maintain a professional and recognizable appearance.

- **Brand Voice and Messaging**: Define your brand's voice and messaging style. Ensure it reflects your brand's personality and resonates with your target audience. Develop key messages and tone guidelines for consistent communication.

3. Brand Experience

- **Customer Touchpoints**: Ensure that every customer touchpoint, from your website and marketing materials to customer support and product interface, aligns with your brand identity. Consistency across touchpoints reinforces your brand image.

- **User Experience**: Design a user experience that reflects your brand values and meets customer expectations. A positive and seamless experience enhances brand perception and loyalty.

- **Customer Service**: Provide exceptional customer service that aligns with your brand's promise. Address customer inquiries and issues promptly and professionally to build trust and satisfaction.

4. Brand Awareness and Advocacy

- **Marketing and Promotion**: Implement marketing strategies to build brand awareness and reach your target audience. Use content marketing, social media, and other channels to communicate your brand message.

- **Brand Advocacy**: Encourage satisfied customers to become brand advocates. Leverage testimonials, case studies, and referrals to build credibility and attract new customers.

- **Monitoring and Adaptation**: Continuously monitor your brand's reputation and performance. Gather feedback from customers and adjust your brand strategy as needed to stay relevant and effective.

By thoroughly understanding your target market and customer personas, and by building a strong, consistent brand identity, you can create a B2B SaaS product that effectively meets customer needs, stands out in the market, and fosters long-term success.

- **Marketing Channels and Strategies for B2B SaaS**

Effective marketing is crucial for the success of a B2B SaaS company. Leveraging the right channels and strategies can help you reach your target audience, generate leads, and drive growth.

1. Content Marketing

- **Blogging**: Create high-quality, relevant blog content that addresses industry challenges, provides solutions, and showcases your expertise. Use SEO best practices to increase visibility and drive organic traffic.

- **Ebooks and Whitepapers**: Develop in-depth resources such as ebooks and whitepapers that offer valuable insights and solutions. Use these as lead magnets to capture contact information from potential customers.

- **Case Studies**: Publish case studies that highlight how your product has successfully addressed challenges for existing clients. This builds credibility and demonstrates the value of your solution.

2. Search Engine Optimization (SEO)

- **Keyword Research**: Identify relevant keywords and phrases that your target audience uses when searching for solutions. Incorporate these keywords into your content and metadata.

- **On-Page SEO**: Optimize your website's pages for search engines by improving meta descriptions, header tags, and internal linking. Ensure your content is valuable and engaging.

- **Technical SEO**: Improve site speed, mobile-friendliness, and ensure proper indexing by search engines. Use tools like Google Search Console to monitor performance and address issues.

3. Social Media Marketing

- **LinkedIn**: Use LinkedIn for professional networking, sharing industry insights, and engaging with decision-makers. Participate in relevant groups and communities to increase visibility.

- **Twitter**: Share updates, thought leadership content, and engage in industry conversations. Use hashtags to reach a broader audience and connect with influencers.

- **Facebook and Instagram**: While less common for B2B, these platforms can be used for brand awareness and showcasing company culture.

4. Email Marketing

- **Newsletters**: Send regular newsletters with updates, valuable content, and product announcements. Segment your email list to tailor content to different audience segments.

- **Drip Campaigns**: Create automated email sequences to nurture leads through the sales funnel. Provide valuable content and gradually introduce your product's benefits.

- **Personalization**: Use personalized email content based on user behavior and interests to increase engagement and conversion rates.

5. Paid Advertising

- **Google Ads**: Use pay-per-click (PPC) advertising to target specific keywords and drive traffic to your website. Set up campaigns with well-defined goals and track performance.

- **LinkedIn Ads**: Utilize LinkedIn's targeting options to reach professionals and decision-makers. Options include sponsored content, InMail, and display ads.

- **Retargeting**: Implement retargeting ads to re-engage visitors who have previously interacted with your website or content. This helps keep your brand top-of-mind and encourages return visits.

6. Webinars and Events

- **Webinars**: Host webinars to provide valuable insights, demonstrate your product, and engage with potential customers. Promote webinars through email, social media, and industry groups.

- **Industry Events**: Participate in or sponsor industry conferences and events. Network with potential customers, partners, and industry experts to build relationships and increase brand visibility.

7. Influencer and Partner Marketing

- **Influencer Partnerships**: Collaborate with industry influencers and thought leaders to promote your product. Influencers can help reach a broader audience and enhance credibility.

- **Partnerships**: Build strategic partnerships with complementary businesses to cross-promote products and services. This can expand your reach and provide additional value to your customers.

Sales Strategies and Building a Sales Team

A strong sales strategy and team are essential for driving revenue and scaling a B2B SaaS business. Here's how to build an effective sales approach and team.

1. Sales Strategies

- **Targeted Outreach**: Focus on high-potential prospects that align with your ideal customer profile (ICP). Use data and research to identify companies and decision-makers who would benefit most from your product.

- **Solution Selling**: Approach sales with a consultative mindset. Understand the prospect's pain points and tailor your pitch to show how your product solves their specific challenges.

- **Account-Based Marketing (ABM)**: Implement ABM strategies to target high-value accounts with personalized marketing and sales efforts. Create tailored content and offers for each account.

- **Sales Funnel Management**: Develop a clear sales funnel with defined stages (e.g., lead generation, qualification, proposal, closing). Use CRM tools to track and manage prospects through the funnel.

- **Customer Success Focus**: Emphasize customer success to drive upsells and renewals. Ensure that existing customers are satisfied and realize the full value of your product.

2. Building a Sales Team

- **Hiring**: Recruit sales professionals with experience in B2B SaaS and a proven track record. Look for candidates who are skilled in consultative selling, relationship building, and have a deep understanding of the industry.

- **Onboarding and Training**: Provide comprehensive onboarding and training programs for new hires. Focus on product knowledge, sales processes, and customer personas to ensure they are well-prepared.

- **Sales Enablement**: Equip your sales team with the tools and resources they need to succeed. This includes CRM systems, sales collateral, and access to relevant market data.

- **Performance Metrics**: Establish clear performance metrics and KPIs to measure the effectiveness of your sales team. Common metrics include conversion rates, sales cycle length, and revenue generated.

- **Incentives and Motivation**: Implement incentive programs to motivate and reward top performers. Offer bonuses, commissions, and other rewards based on achieving sales targets and driving revenue.

- **Continuous Improvement**: Foster a culture of continuous improvement by providing ongoing training and development opportunities. Encourage feedback and adapt strategies based on performance and market changes.

3. Sales Process Optimization

- **Lead Qualification**: Implement a lead qualification process to ensure that sales efforts are focused on high-potential prospects. Use criteria such as budget, authority, need, and timing (BANT) or other frameworks.

- **Sales Playbooks**: Develop sales playbooks that outline best practices, scripts, and tactics for different stages of the sales process. This ensures consistency and efficiency in sales activities.

- **Customer Feedback**: Gather feedback from prospects and customers to refine your sales approach. Use this feedback to address objections, improve messaging, and enhance the sales experience.

By leveraging effective marketing channels and strategies, and by building a skilled sales team with a well-defined sales strategy, you can drive growth, attract and retain customers, and achieve success in the competitive B2B SaaS market.

- **Measuring and Analyzing Your Marketing and Sales Efforts**

Measuring and analyzing your marketing and sales efforts is crucial for understanding what's working, identifying areas for improvement, and optimizing your strategies for better results. Here's a guide to effectively track and analyze your marketing and sales performance:

1. Key Performance Indicators (KPIs)

Marketing KPIs:

- **Website Traffic**: Track the number of visitors to your website. Use tools like Google Analytics to monitor traffic sources, user behavior, and page performance.

- **Lead Generation**: Measure the number of leads generated from different marketing channels (e.g., email campaigns, content marketing, social media). Assess lead quality and conversion rates.

- **Conversion Rate**: Calculate the percentage of visitors who complete a desired action, such as signing up for a trial or filling out a contact form. This helps gauge the effectiveness of your landing pages and calls-to-action (CTAs).

- **Cost Per Lead (CPL)**: Determine the cost of acquiring each lead by dividing your total marketing spend by the number of leads generated. This helps evaluate the efficiency of your marketing campaigns.

- **Return on Investment (ROI)**: Measure the ROI of your marketing activities by comparing the revenue generated from marketing efforts to the costs incurred. This helps assess the overall effectiveness of your marketing spend.

Sales KPIs:

- **Sales Revenue**: Track the total revenue generated from sales activities. Monitor revenue growth over time and compare it against targets.

- **Sales Conversion Rate**: Calculate the percentage of leads that convert into paying customers. This helps evaluate the effectiveness of your sales team and processes.

- **Average Deal Size**: Measure the average value of each sale. This helps assess the profitability of your sales and identify opportunities for upselling or cross-selling.

- **Sales Cycle Length**: Track the average time it takes to close a deal from initial contact to final sale. Shortening the sales cycle can improve efficiency and increase revenue.

- **Customer Acquisition Cost (CAC)**: Determine the cost of acquiring a new customer by dividing your total sales and marketing expenses by the number of new customers acquired. This helps evaluate the efficiency of your acquisition efforts.

2. Data Collection and Analysis

Analytics Tools:

- **Google Analytics**: Use Google Analytics to track website traffic, user behavior, and conversion metrics. Set up goals and funnels to measure specific actions and performance.

- **CRM Systems**: Utilize Customer Relationship Management (CRM) systems like Salesforce or HubSpot to track sales activities, manage leads, and analyze customer interactions and performance.

- **Marketing Automation Platforms**: Implement marketing automation tools (e.g., Marketo, Pardot) to track campaign performance, lead nurturing, and customer engagement.

Data Analysis:

- **Trend Analysis**: Analyze trends in your marketing and sales data over time. Look for patterns or changes in performance metrics to identify opportunities or areas of concern.

- **Segmentation**: Segment your data by different factors (e.g., lead source, customer segment) to gain insights into how different groups perform and identify targeted strategies.

- **Benchmarking**: Compare your performance metrics against industry benchmarks or competitors. This helps assess your relative performance and identify areas for improvement.

3. Reporting and Optimization

Reporting:

- **Regular Reports**: Generate regular reports (e.g., weekly, monthly) to review marketing and sales performance. Include key metrics, trends, and insights to evaluate progress and make informed decisions.

- **Dashboards**: Create visual dashboards to provide real-time visibility into your marketing and sales performance. Use tools like Tableau or Google Data Studio to display key metrics and trends.

Optimization:

- **A/B Testing**: Conduct A/B testing on marketing campaigns, landing pages, and sales tactics to determine what works best. Test different variations and analyze results to optimize performance.

- **Feedback Loop**: Implement a feedback loop to continuously gather input from customers, sales teams, and marketing staff. Use this feedback to make data-driven improvements and refine strategies.

- **Adjust Strategies**: Based on your analysis, adjust your marketing and sales strategies as needed. Optimize campaigns, refine targeting, and improve processes to enhance overall performance.

By systematically measuring and analyzing your marketing and sales efforts, you can gain valuable insights, optimize your strategies, and drive better results. This data-driven approach helps ensure that your efforts are aligned with your goals and delivers the best possible return on investment.

CHAPTER 5

SCALING YOUR SAAS BUSINESS

Identifying growth opportunities and understanding potential challenges is essential for scaling a B2B SaaS business effectively. Here's how to approach this process:

1. Identifying Growth Opportunities

Market Expansion:

- **New Markets**: Explore opportunities to enter new geographic regions or verticals. Conduct market research to understand demand, competition, and regulatory requirements in potential new markets.

- **Market Trends**: Stay informed about industry trends and emerging technologies. Identify trends that align with your product and can drive growth, such as advances in AI, data analytics, or remote work solutions.

Product Innovation:

- **Feature Enhancements**: Evaluate opportunities to enhance your product with new features or functionalities that meet evolving customer needs. Gather feedback from existing customers to identify areas for improvement.

- **Technology Integration**: Consider integrating with other popular platforms or technologies to increase your product's value and appeal. For example, integrating with CRM systems, analytics tools, or collaboration platforms can provide additional benefits to users.

Customer Segmentation:

- **Upselling and Cross-Selling**: Identify opportunities to upsell premium features or cross-sell complementary products to existing customers. Develop targeted offers and marketing campaigns to drive additional revenue.

- **Customer Success Programs**: Implement customer success programs to identify and nurture high-value accounts. Offer tailored support and resources to enhance their experience and encourage long-term retention.

Strategic Partnerships:

- **Channel Partnerships**: Develop partnerships with other companies or resellers that can help distribute your product to new customer segments or geographic regions. Consider joint ventures or affiliate programs to expand your reach.

- **Industry Alliances**: Collaborate with industry associations, thought leaders, or influencers to enhance your brand visibility and credibility. Participate in industry events or contribute to relevant publications.

2. Addressing Challenges

Competitive Pressure:

- **Competitive Analysis**: Continuously monitor competitors' offerings, pricing, and strategies. Identify your unique value proposition and differentiation points to stay ahead of the competition.

- **Adaptation**: Be prepared to adapt your strategies and product features in response to competitive threats. Stay agile and responsive to changes in the market landscape.

Customer Retention:

- **Churn Analysis**: Analyze customer churn rates to understand why customers are leaving. Gather feedback from departing customers to identify issues and improve your product or service.

- **Retention Strategies**: Implement strategies to enhance customer satisfaction and loyalty. This can include personalized customer support, loyalty programs, and regular engagement through content or updates.

Scalability:

- **Infrastructure**: Ensure that your technical infrastructure can handle increased demand as you scale. Invest in scalable cloud services, load balancing, and monitoring tools to maintain performance and reliability.

- **Operational Efficiency**: Streamline operations to manage growth effectively. Automate processes where possible, and optimize workflows to ensure efficient use of resources.

Financial Management:

•   **Cash Flow**: Monitor cash flow closely to ensure you have sufficient funds to support growth initiatives. Develop financial projections and manage expenses to avoid potential cash flow issues.

•   **Funding**: Explore additional funding options if needed to support expansion plans. Consider venture capital, strategic investors, or alternative financing methods to fuel growth.

Expanding Your Product Offerings

Expanding your product offerings can drive growth by attracting new customers, increasing revenue, and enhancing customer satisfaction. Here's how to approach product expansion:

1. Assessing Market Needs

•   **Customer Feedback**: Gather feedback from existing customers to identify gaps in your current offerings and understand their evolving needs. Use surveys, interviews, and support interactions to collect insights.

•   **Market Research**: Conduct market research to identify trends, customer pain points, and opportunities for new products or features. Analyze competitor offerings to determine potential areas for differentiation.

2. Developing New Products or Features

•   **Idea Generation**: Generate ideas for new products or features based on market research and customer feedback. Involve

60

your team in brainstorming sessions and prioritize ideas based on potential impact and feasibility.

- **Validation**: Validate new product ideas through prototype testing or pilot programs. Gather feedback from a small group of customers to assess interest and viability before full-scale development.

- **Product Roadmap**: Develop a product roadmap that outlines the development timeline, key milestones, and resource requirements for new products or features. Ensure alignment with your overall business strategy and goals.

3. Launching and Marketing New Offerings

- **Launch Strategy**: Develop a launch strategy that includes messaging, pricing, and promotional activities. Create a marketing plan to generate buzz and drive adoption of the new product or feature.

- **Customer Education**: Provide resources and training to help customers understand and use the new offering effectively. This can include tutorials, webinars, or documentation.

- **Feedback and Iteration**: Monitor the performance of new products or features and gather feedback from users. Use this feedback to make improvements and address any issues.

4. Integration and Bundling

- **Product Integration**: Consider integrating new products or features with your existing offerings to provide a seamless experience for customers. Ensure compatibility and ease of use.

- **Bundling**: Offer bundled packages that combine multiple products or features at a discounted price. This can encourage customers to purchase more and increase overall revenue.

5. Scaling and Support

- **Infrastructure**: Ensure that your infrastructure can support the additional load from new products or features. Invest in scalable technology and support systems to handle increased demand.

- **Customer Support**: Provide adequate support for new products or features to assist customers with any issues or questions. Train your support team to handle inquiries and troubleshoot problems effectively.

By identifying growth opportunities, addressing challenges, and expanding your product offerings strategically, you can drive sustained growth and success for your B2B SaaS business.

- **Scaling Your Operations and Infrastructure**

Scaling operations and infrastructure is crucial for managing growth and maintaining service quality as your B2B SaaS company expands. Here's how to approach scaling effectively:

1. Infrastructure Scaling

Cloud Services:

- **Scalable Cloud Solutions**: Utilize cloud services that offer scalability, such as Amazon Web Services (AWS), Microsoft Azure, or Google Cloud Platform. These platforms provide on-demand resources that can scale up or down based on your needs.

- **Load Balancing**: Implement load balancers to distribute incoming traffic evenly across multiple servers. This helps prevent server overloads and ensures consistent performance.

Database Management:

- **Scalable Databases**: Choose databases that can handle increased data volumes and user loads. Consider options like Amazon RDS, Google Cloud SQL, or distributed databases like Cassandra or MongoDB.

- **Data Replication and Backup**: Implement data replication and backup strategies to ensure data availability and protection. Regularly test your backup and recovery processes.

Performance Monitoring:

- **Monitoring Tools**: Use performance monitoring tools like New Relic, Datadog, or Prometheus to track application performance, identify bottlenecks, and ensure system reliability.

- **Alerts and Automation**: Set up alerts for performance issues and automate responses to common problems. This helps maintain system stability and reduces downtime.

2. Operational Scaling

Process Automation:

- **Automate Repetitive Tasks**: Identify repetitive tasks that can be automated, such as billing, user provisioning, or reporting. Use tools like Zapier or custom scripts to streamline these processes.

- **Workflow Optimization**: Optimize workflows to improve efficiency and reduce manual effort. Document and standardize processes to ensure consistency and ease of scaling.

Resource Management:

- **Capacity Planning**: Regularly assess your resource needs based on growth projections and historical data. Plan for additional capacity in advance to avoid disruptions.

- **Vendor Management**: Manage relationships with vendors and service providers to ensure they can meet your scaling needs. Negotiate contracts that allow for flexibility as your requirements change.

Cost Management:

- **Budgeting**: Develop a budget that accounts for scaling costs, such as additional cloud resources, infrastructure upgrades, and process improvements.

- **Cost Optimization**: Regularly review and optimize your expenses. Look for cost-saving opportunities, such as reserved instances for cloud services or more efficient resource allocation.

Building a Scalable Customer Support System

A scalable customer support system is essential for maintaining customer satisfaction and managing increased support demands as your business grows. Here's how to build and scale your support system effectively:

1. Support Channels

Multichannel Support:

- **Omnichannel Strategy**: Provide support across multiple channels, such as email, chat, phone, and social media. Ensure a consistent experience across all channels.

- **Self-Service Options**: Implement self-service options like knowledge bases, FAQs, and community forums. This allows customers to find answers independently and reduces the volume of support requests.

Support Tools:

- **Helpdesk Software**: Use helpdesk software like Zendesk, Freshdesk, or ServiceNow to manage and track support tickets, assign tasks, and monitor performance.

- **Live Chat Tools**: Implement live chat tools to provide real-time assistance and improve customer engagement. Use tools like Intercom or Drift for chat-based support.

2. Team Structure and Training

Support Team Structure:

- **Tiered Support**: Organize your support team into tiers based on expertise. Frontline agents handle basic issues, while more experienced agents or specialists address complex problems.

- **Team Roles**: Define clear roles and responsibilities for each team member, including support agents, team leads, and managers. Ensure effective communication and collaboration.

Training and Development:

- **Onboarding**: Provide comprehensive onboarding training for new support team members. Cover product knowledge, support processes, and customer interaction best practices.

- **Continuous Training**: Offer ongoing training and professional development opportunities. Keep your team updated on new features, industry trends, and customer service skills.

3. Performance Monitoring and Improvement

Metrics and KPIs:

- **Customer Satisfaction (CSAT)**: Measure customer satisfaction through surveys and feedback. Use this data to identify areas for improvement and enhance the support experience.

- **First Response Time**: Track the average time it takes for support agents to respond to customer inquiries. Aim to reduce response times and improve efficiency.

Feedback and Iteration:

- **Customer Feedback**: Gather feedback from customers about their support experience. Use this feedback to make improvements and address common issues.

- **Process Improvement**: Regularly review and optimize support processes. Implement changes based on performance data and feedback to enhance efficiency and customer satisfaction.

Hiring and Retaining Top Talent

Attracting and retaining top talent is crucial for building a strong team and driving growth in your B2B SaaS company. Here's how to approach hiring and retention effectively:

1. Hiring Top Talent

Recruitment Strategy:

- **Talent Pool**: Build a talent pool by networking, attending industry events, and engaging with potential candidates through social media and job boards.

- **Job Descriptions**: Create clear and compelling job descriptions that outline the role, responsibilities, and required qualifications. Highlight your company's culture and benefits.

Interview Process:

- **Structured Interviews**: Use structured interviews with standardized questions to assess candidates' skills, experience, and cultural fit. Include technical assessments and problem-solving exercises.

- **Team Involvement**: Involve team members in the interview process to assess candidates from different perspectives. Ensure alignment with team dynamics and company values.

Onboarding:

- **Effective Onboarding**: Develop a comprehensive onboarding program that includes training, orientation, and introductions to key team members. Ensure new hires have the resources and support they need to succeed.

2. Retaining Top Talent

Career Development:

- **Growth Opportunities**: Provide opportunities for career growth and advancement. Offer mentorship, training, and development programs to help employees reach their career goals.

- **Recognition and Rewards**: Recognize and reward employees for their contributions and achievements. Implement programs such as employee of the month, performance bonuses, and peer recognition.

Work Environment:

- **Positive Culture**: Foster a positive and inclusive company culture that values teamwork, innovation, and open communication. Encourage collaboration and support a healthy work-life balance.

- **Feedback and Support**: Regularly solicit feedback from employees and address any concerns or issues. Provide support and resources to help employees succeed and stay engaged.

Compensation and Benefits:

- **Competitive Salaries**: Offer competitive salaries and compensation packages based on industry standards and employee experience. Regularly review and adjust compensation as needed.

- **Benefits Package**: Provide a comprehensive benefits package that includes health insurance, retirement plans, and other perks. Consider offering flexible work arrangements or remote work options.

Employee Engagement:

- **Regular Check-Ins**: Conduct regular one-on-one meetings with employees to discuss their progress, career goals, and any challenges they may be facing. Use these meetings to provide feedback and support.

- **Team Building**: Organize team-building activities and events to strengthen relationships and improve team cohesion. Encourage social interactions and collaboration outside of work.

By effectively scaling your operations and infrastructure, building a scalable customer support system, and hiring and retaining top talent, you can support your B2B SaaS company's growth and ensure long-term success.

CHAPTER 6
IMPLEMENTING EFFECTIVE PRICING MODELS

Selecting the right pricing model is crucial for a SaaS business, as it can significantly impact revenue, customer acquisition, and retention. Here's an overview of the most common SaaS pricing models:

1. Subscription-Based Pricing

Monthly or Annual Subscriptions:

- **Description**: Customers pay a recurring fee on a monthly or annual basis to access the software. This is the most common SaaS pricing model.

- **Benefits**: Predictable revenue stream, easier customer retention, and simplified billing.

- **Considerations**: Offer discounts for annual subscriptions to encourage longer commitments and reduce churn.

2. Freemium Model

Free Tier with Paid Upgrades:

- **Description**: Provides a basic version of the software for free while offering premium features or functionality for a fee.

- **Benefits**: Attracts a large user base and allows potential customers to experience the product before committing to a paid plan.

- **Considerations**: Balance between free and paid features to encourage upgrades without diminishing the value of the free tier.

3. Usage-Based Pricing

Pay-As-You-Go:

- **Description**: Customers pay based on their usage of the software, such as the number of transactions, data storage, or API calls.

- **Benefits**: Aligns pricing with customer value and usage, which can be attractive to businesses with fluctuating needs.

- **Considerations**: Requires robust tracking and reporting systems to accurately measure and bill usage.

4. Tiered Pricing

Multiple Pricing Plans:

- **Description**: Offers several pricing tiers with different levels of features, functionality, or usage limits. Customers choose the plan that best fits their needs.

- **Benefits**: Provides flexibility and options for different customer segments. Encourages customers to move up to higher tiers for more features.

- **Considerations**: Clearly define the value and features included in each tier to avoid confusion and ensure customers perceive the value.

5. Per-User Pricing

Pricing Based on Number of Users:

- **Description**: Charges customers based on the number of users or seats accessing the software.

- **Benefits**: Simple to understand and scalable as organizations grow. Can be effective for collaborative or team-based software.

- **Considerations**: Consider offering volume discounts or caps to address large organizations and encourage adoption.

6. Flat-Rate Pricing

Single Price for All Features:

- **Description**: A single, fixed price grants access to all features and functionality of the software.

- **Benefits**: Simple and straightforward pricing that's easy for customers to understand. Eliminates confusion over feature availability.

- **Considerations**: May limit revenue potential from customers who are willing to pay more for additional features.

7. Per-Feature Pricing

Pricing Based on Feature Set:

- **Description**: Charges customers based on the specific features or modules they use, allowing them to select and pay for only the features they need.

- **Benefits**: Allows for customized solutions and can attract customers with specific needs.

- **Considerations**: Complexity in pricing structure and potential for customer confusion. Ensure clear communication of feature value.

8. Pay-Per-Transaction

Pricing Based on Transactions or Actions:

- **Description**: Customers pay based on the number of transactions, actions, or events they perform using the software.

- **Benefits**: Aligns costs with the value derived from the software. Suitable for platforms where usage is variable.

- **Considerations**: Requires accurate tracking and billing systems. Potentially unpredictable costs for customers.

How to Choose the Right Pricing Model for Your Business

Choosing the right pricing model for your SaaS business depends on several factors, including your target market, product features, and revenue goals. Here's a step-by-step guide to help you make an informed decision:

1. Understand Your Customers

Customer Segmentation:

- **Identify Customer Needs**: Understand the needs and preferences of different customer segments. Consider their willingness to pay, feature requirements, and usage patterns.

- **Customer Feedback**: Gather feedback from potential and existing customers to determine their pricing expectations and preferences.

Value Perception:

- **Assess Value**: Evaluate how your software provides value to customers. Different models align better with different types of value, such as cost savings, productivity improvements, or revenue generation.

2. Analyze Your Product

Feature Complexity:

- **Feature Set**: Consider the complexity and range of features your software offers. Models like tiered or per-feature pricing can accommodate varying levels of functionality.

- **Usage Patterns**: Analyze how customers use your software. Usage-based or pay-per-transaction models may be suitable for products with variable or intensive usage.

Scalability:

- **Growth Potential**: Choose a pricing model that supports your growth strategy. For example, subscription models provide predictable revenue, while usage-based models scale with customer engagement.

3. Evaluate Financial Implications

Revenue Forecasting:

• **Revenue Projections**: Estimate potential revenue under different pricing models. Consider factors like customer acquisition costs, churn rates, and pricing elasticity.

• **Profit Margins**: Analyze how each model impacts profit margins. Ensure the model supports your business's financial goals and sustainability.

Cost Considerations:

• **Operational Costs**: Evaluate how each pricing model impacts operational costs, such as billing, support, and infrastructure. Choose a model that aligns with your cost structure and operational capacity.

4. Consider Market Positioning

Competitive Analysis:

• **Market Research**: Analyze the pricing models used by competitors. Determine how your pricing model compares and what differentiates your offering.

• **Positioning Strategy**: Align your pricing model with your market positioning and brand strategy. Ensure it reflects the perceived value and competitive advantage of your product.

5. Test and Iterate

Pilot Testing:

- **Test Models**: Consider running pilot tests or A/B tests with different pricing models to gather real-world data on customer preferences and behavior.

- **Iterate**: Be prepared to adjust your pricing model based on feedback and performance. Continuous iteration helps optimize pricing and maximize revenue.

Customer Communication:

- **Clear Messaging**: Communicate the value and rationale behind your pricing model clearly to customers. Ensure transparency and address any questions or concerns.

By carefully evaluating these factors and testing different models, you can choose the pricing strategy that best fits your SaaS business, aligns with customer needs, and supports your growth objectives.

- **Psychology of Pricing and Customer Perception**

Understanding the psychology of pricing and how it affects customer perception can significantly impact your SaaS business's success. Here's how different pricing strategies and psychological principles can influence customer behavior:

1. Price Anchoring

Definition:

- **Price Anchoring**: The concept of setting a reference price (anchor) to influence customers' perception of value. Customers compare the anchor price to other prices to assess value.

Application:

- **High-Price Anchor**: Introduce a higher-priced plan or product to make other options seem more affordable in comparison. This can make your mid-tier or standard plans appear more attractive.

- **Discount Anchoring**: Use discounts or promotions to create a sense of urgency and highlight savings. For example, showing a "discounted from $99 to $59" can make the lower price seem like a better deal.

2. Perceived Value Pricing

Definition:

- **Perceived Value Pricing**: Pricing based on the perceived value of the product to the customer rather than the cost of production or market rates.

Application:

- **Value-Based Pricing**: Set prices according to the value customers believe they are receiving. This requires understanding customer needs, pain points, and how much they value your solution.

- **Feature Differentiation**: Clearly communicate the unique benefits and features of your product. Ensure that customers understand the value they are receiving compared to alternatives.

3. Pricing Tiers and Choice Overload

Definition:

• **Choice Overload**: Too many options can overwhelm customers and lead to decision paralysis. Simplifying choices can improve customer satisfaction and increase conversions.

Application:

• **Tiered Pricing**: Offer a limited number of pricing tiers (e.g., basic, standard, premium) to simplify choices. Ensure each tier provides clear value and distinct features.

• **Default Option**: Highlight a recommended or default option in your pricing plans. This can guide customers towards a choice that aligns with their needs and maximize conversions.

4. Psychological Pricing Strategies

Definition:

• **Psychological Pricing**: Techniques that leverage psychological principles to influence customer perceptions and purchasing decisions.

Application:

• **Charm Pricing**: Use prices ending in .99 or .95 (e.g., $99.99) to create the perception of a better deal. This is based on the idea that prices just below a round number seem significantly lower.

• **Bundling**: Offer product bundles at a discount compared to purchasing items individually. This can increase perceived value and encourage customers to buy more.

5. Subscription Pricing and Customer Commitment

Definition:

• **Subscription Pricing**: Regular payments for ongoing access to a product or service. This model influences customer perceptions of value and commitment.

Application:

• **Free Trials**: Offer free trials or freemium models to allow customers to experience the product before committing. This builds trust and lowers the barrier to entry.

• **Annual Plans**: Provide discounts for annual subscriptions compared to monthly payments. This encourages long-term commitment and improves customer retention.

Testing and Iterating Your Pricing Strategy

To ensure that your pricing strategy is effective and aligns with customer expectations, it's crucial to test and iterate. Here's a structured approach to testing and refining your pricing strategy:

1. A/B Testing

Definition:

• **A/B Testing**: Comparing two or more versions of your pricing strategy to determine which performs better.

Application:

• **Test Variables**: Experiment with different pricing models, tiers, or promotional offers. For example, test different price points or bundle options to see which generates more conversions or revenue.

- **Analyze Results**: Use metrics such as conversion rates, average revenue per user (ARPU), and customer acquisition cost (CAC) to evaluate the effectiveness of each pricing variation.

2. Customer Feedback and Surveys

Definition:

- **Customer Feedback**: Collecting insights from customers about their perceptions and experiences with your pricing.

Application:

- **Surveys and Interviews**: Conduct surveys or interviews with current and potential customers to gather feedback on pricing preferences, perceived value, and willingness to pay.

- **Feedback Analysis**: Analyze feedback to identify common themes and areas for improvement. Use this information to refine your pricing strategy.

3. Competitive Analysis

Definition:

- **Competitive Analysis**: Evaluating competitors' pricing strategies and positioning to understand market dynamics and identify opportunities.

Application:

- **Benchmarking**: Compare your pricing with competitors to ensure it is competitive and aligns with market expectations. Identify gaps or opportunities for differentiation.

- **Market Positioning**: Assess how your pricing positions you relative to competitors. Ensure that your pricing reflects your unique value proposition and target market positioning.

4. Revenue and Financial Metrics

Definition:

- **Revenue Metrics**: Monitoring financial performance indicators to assess the impact of pricing changes.

Application:

- **Monitor Metrics**: Track key metrics such as revenue growth, customer lifetime value (CLV), and churn rates. Evaluate how pricing changes affect these metrics.

- **Adjust Pricing**: Use financial data to make informed adjustments to your pricing strategy. Ensure that changes align with your revenue and profitability goals.

5. Continuous Iteration

Definition:

- **Continuous Iteration**: Regularly updating and refining your pricing strategy based on testing results, feedback, and market changes.

Application:

- **Iterative Process**: Implement changes incrementally and monitor their impact. Use insights from testing and feedback to make ongoing adjustments and improvements.

- **Adapt to Changes**: Stay responsive to market trends, customer preferences, and competitive dynamics. Continuously refine your pricing strategy to maintain relevance and competitiveness.

By understanding the psychology of pricing and continuously testing and iterating your pricing strategy, you can optimize your SaaS pricing model to better meet customer needs, maximize revenue, and drive business growth.

- **Case Studies of Successful Pricing Models**

Examining real-world examples of successful pricing models can provide valuable insights into how different strategies can drive growth and optimize revenue. Here are case studies from prominent SaaS companies that have effectively implemented various pricing models:

1. Salesforce: Subscription-Based Pricing

Company Overview: Salesforce is a leading CRM (Customer Relationship Management) platform that offers a range of cloud-based applications for sales, customer service, and marketing.

Pricing Model: Salesforce utilizes a subscription-based pricing model with multiple tiers. Their pricing structure includes various plans, such as Essentials, Professional, Enterprise, and Unlimited, each offering different levels of functionality and support.

Key Success Factors:

- **Tiered Plans**: The tiered pricing model allows Salesforce to cater to businesses of all sizes, from small startups to large enterprises. Each tier provides different features and levels of customization, enabling customers to choose a plan that fits their needs and budget.

- **Predictable Revenue**: The subscription model provides Salesforce with a predictable and recurring revenue stream, which is crucial for sustaining growth and investing in product development.

- **Upselling Opportunities**: The structured tiers create opportunities for upselling and cross-selling. As businesses grow or require additional features, they are incentivized to move to higher-tier plans.

Outcome: Salesforce's subscription-based pricing model has been instrumental in its growth, contributing to its status as one of the largest SaaS companies globally. The model supports consistent revenue generation and helps the company maintain a high level of customer engagement.

2. Slack: Freemium Model

Company Overview: Slack is a collaboration and messaging platform designed to enhance team communication and productivity.

Pricing Model: Slack employs a freemium pricing model, offering a basic version of its product for free while providing premium features through paid plans like Standard, Plus, and Enterprise Grid.

Key Success Factors:

• **Wide User Base**: The free tier allows users to experience Slack's core functionalities without any initial investment. This helps attract a large user base and encourages widespread adoption.

• **Conversion to Paid Plans**: The freemium model drives conversions by offering additional features and benefits in the paid tiers, such as enhanced security, larger file storage, and advanced administrative tools.

• **Product Engagement**: Users who find value in the free version are more likely to upgrade to paid plans as their needs grow. This gradual conversion approach supports scalable growth.

Outcome: Slack's freemium model has been highly successful in growing its user base and driving revenue. The company's ability to attract a large number of users and convert a significant portion to paid plans has contributed to its rapid expansion and market dominance.

3. HubSpot: Tiered and Freemium Pricing

Company Overview: HubSpot provides a suite of marketing, sales, and customer service software designed to help businesses grow and manage their operations.

Pricing Model: HubSpot uses a combination of freemium and tiered pricing models. It offers a free CRM and a suite of free tools, with advanced features available through various paid plans, including Starter, Professional, and Enterprise.

Key Success Factors:

- **Freemium Model for Entry**: HubSpot's free tools serve as an entry point for new customers. The free version helps businesses get started and understand the value of HubSpot's offerings.

- **Tiered Upgrades**: The tiered pricing structure provides options for businesses to scale and access advanced features as they grow. This encourages long-term customer relationships and continuous revenue growth.

- **Comprehensive Suite**: Offering a full suite of integrated tools across different tiers supports a seamless customer experience and enhances cross-selling opportunities.

Outcome: HubSpot's hybrid pricing model has been effective in attracting a wide range of customers, from small businesses to large enterprises. The model supports customer acquisition, retention, and growth, driving HubSpot's success in the competitive SaaS market.

4. Zoom: Usage-Based Pricing

Company Overview: Zoom is a video conferencing and communication platform used for meetings, webinars, and online collaboration.

Pricing Model: Zoom's pricing model includes both subscription and usage-based elements. The platform offers a range of plans, from a free basic plan with limited features to paid plans like Pro, Business, and Enterprise. Zoom also charges based on usage for certain features, such as webinar hosting.

Key Success Factors:

- **Flexible Plans**: Zoom's subscription plans provide flexibility for different types of users, from individual professionals to large organizations. The usage-based pricing for add-ons and features allows customers to pay based on their specific needs.

- **High Adoption Rates**: The free plan and usage-based model have contributed to Zoom's widespread adoption and ease of entry. Users can start with minimal investment and scale as needed.

- **Scalability**: The combination of subscription and usage-based pricing supports scalability, allowing Zoom to accommodate a growing number of users and usage scenarios.

Outcome: Zoom's pricing model has played a key role in its rapid growth and market penetration. The model's flexibility and accessibility have contributed to Zoom's success as a leading video conferencing solution.

5. Atlassian: Per-User and Tiered Pricing

Company Overview: Atlassian is a provider of collaboration and productivity software, including tools like Jira, Confluence, and Trello.

Pricing Model: Atlassian employs a per-user pricing model for many of its products, combined with tiered pricing for additional features and support. For example, Jira offers different plans based on the number of users and features required, with pricing increasing as user numbers grow.

Key Success Factors:

- **Per-User Pricing**: The per-user model aligns costs with the number of users, making it scalable for both small teams and large enterprises. This model supports predictable revenue and aligns pricing with customer growth.

- **Tiered Upgrades**: Additional tiers offer enhanced features and support, providing clear value for businesses looking to expand their usage or require more advanced capabilities.

- **Freemium Entry**: Some Atlassian products, like Trello, offer free versions with basic features, encouraging adoption and driving upgrades to paid plans.

Outcome: Atlassian's pricing strategy has supported its growth by accommodating a diverse customer base and providing scalable solutions. The combination of per-user and tiered pricing has been effective in driving revenue and expanding market reach.

These case studies illustrate how different pricing models can be successfully implemented in the SaaS industry. By aligning pricing strategies with customer needs, market positioning, and product features, companies like Salesforce, Slack, HubSpot, Zoom, and Atlassian have effectively driven growth and optimized revenue. Each model has its strengths and applications, and selecting the right approach depends on various factors, including customer preferences, product complexity, and business goals.

CHAPTER 7
CUSTOMER RETENTION AND SUCCESS

Customer Retention is a critical metric for SaaS businesses due to its direct impact on revenue, growth, and overall business health. Here's why it's so important:

1. Recurring Revenue

- **Predictable Income**: SaaS models typically rely on subscription-based revenue. Retaining customers ensures a steady stream of recurring revenue, which is crucial for long-term financial stability.

- **Revenue Growth**: Retained customers are more likely to upgrade their plans or purchase additional features, contributing to revenue growth without the high costs of acquiring new customers.

2. Customer Lifetime Value (CLV)

- **Increased CLV**: The longer a customer stays, the higher their lifetime value. This metric reflects the total revenue a business can expect from a customer throughout their relationship.

- **Cost Efficiency**: Retaining existing customers is generally more cost-effective than acquiring new ones. Lower churn rates improve CLV and reduce the overall cost of customer acquisition.

3. Positive Word-of-Mouth and Referrals

- **Customer Advocacy**: Satisfied, long-term customers are more likely to recommend your product to others, leading to valuable word-of-mouth referrals.

- **Enhanced Reputation**: High retention rates can build a positive brand reputation, which is crucial for attracting new customers and establishing trust in the market.

4. Reduced Churn Rates

- **Minimized Losses**: High churn rates can significantly impact revenue and growth. Retention strategies help reduce churn, ensuring that customers remain engaged and satisfied with your product.

- **Predictable Growth**: Lower churn rates contribute to more predictable business growth and stability, making it easier to plan for the future.

5. Improved Product Development

- **Customer Feedback**: Long-term customers provide valuable feedback on product features and performance. This input is crucial for ongoing product improvements and innovation.

- **Feature Adoption**: Retained customers are more likely to use and benefit from new features, which can drive further engagement and satisfaction.

Strategies for Improving Customer Onboarding

Effective customer onboarding is essential for ensuring a positive first impression and setting the stage for long-term success. Here are some strategies to improve your onboarding process:

1. Simplify the Onboarding Process

- **Clear Instructions**: Provide clear, step-by-step instructions for getting started with your product. Avoid overwhelming new users with too much information at once.

- **User-Friendly Interface**: Design an intuitive onboarding experience with user-friendly interfaces and easy navigation to minimize friction and confusion.

2. Personalized Onboarding Experience

- **Tailored Guidance**: Customize the onboarding process based on the user's role, industry, or use case. Offer relevant tutorials and resources that align with their specific needs.

- **Personal Touch**: Assign onboarding specialists or provide personalized support to guide new users through the setup and initial usage.

3. Interactive Onboarding Tools

- **Walkthroughs and Tutorials**: Use interactive walkthroughs, tutorials, and in-app guides to help users understand key features and functionalities.

- **Product Tours**: Offer product tours that highlight important features and demonstrate how they can be used effectively.

4. Provide Easy Access to Resources

- **Knowledge Base**: Create a comprehensive knowledge base with articles, videos, and FAQs that users can access at any time.

- **Customer Support**: Offer easy access to customer support through chat, email, or phone to address any questions or issues during the onboarding process.

5. Set Clear Expectations

- **Onboarding Goals**: Define clear onboarding goals and milestones to help users understand what they should achieve and by when.

- **Progress Tracking**: Provide progress indicators or checklists to help users track their onboarding journey and stay motivated.

6. Gather and Act on Feedback

- **User Surveys**: Collect feedback from new users about their onboarding experience to identify areas for improvement.

- **Iterative Improvements**: Use feedback to make iterative improvements to your onboarding process and address any common pain points.

Implementing a Customer Success Program

A Customer Success Program focuses on ensuring that customers achieve their desired outcomes and derive maximum value from your product. Here's how to implement an effective program:

1. Define Customer Success Metrics

- **Key Metrics**: Identify key metrics for measuring customer success, such as customer satisfaction (CSAT), net promoter score (NPS), customer lifetime value (CLV), and retention rates.

- **Success Criteria**: Establish clear criteria for what constitutes a successful customer outcome and use these criteria to guide your program.

2. Build a Customer Success Team

- **Dedicated Roles**: Hire or assign dedicated customer success managers (CSMs) who are responsible for nurturing customer relationships and ensuring their success.

- **Training and Tools**: Equip your team with the necessary training and tools to effectively manage customer relationships and address their needs.

3. Develop a Customer Success Strategy

- **Proactive Engagement**: Implement a proactive approach to customer success by regularly reaching out to customers, offering support, and identifying opportunities for improvement.

- **Customer Journey Mapping**: Map out the customer journey to understand key touchpoints and ensure that customers receive support at critical stages.

4. Implement Regular Check-Ins and Reviews

- **Periodic Check-Ins**: Schedule regular check-ins with customers to review their progress, address any issues, and discuss opportunities for further engagement.

- **Quarterly Business Reviews (QBRs)**: Conduct QBRs to assess overall performance, share insights, and align on goals for the upcoming period.

5. Provide Value-Added Services

- **Training and Workshops**: Offer training sessions, workshops, or webinars to help customers maximize their use of your product.

- **Best Practices**: Share best practices, tips, and resources to help customers optimize their usage and achieve their desired outcomes.

6. Foster a Customer-Centric Culture

- **Customer Feedback Loop**: Create a feedback loop where customer insights and suggestions are regularly collected and acted upon.

- **Cross-Functional Collaboration**: Ensure collaboration between customer success, product development, and support teams to address customer needs and improve the product.

7. Monitor and Adapt

- **Continuous Improvement**: Regularly assess the effectiveness of your customer success program and make adjustments based on feedback and performance metrics.

94

- **Scalable Solutions**: Develop scalable solutions and processes to ensure that your customer success program can grow with your business.

By focusing on customer retention, optimizing onboarding processes, and implementing a robust customer success program, SaaS businesses can enhance customer satisfaction, drive long-term engagement, and achieve sustainable growth.

- **Using Data and Analytics to Enhance Customer Satisfaction**

Leveraging data and analytics is crucial for improving customer satisfaction in a SaaS business. By understanding customer behavior and preferences, you can make informed decisions and tailor your strategies to meet their needs. Here's how to effectively use data and analytics to enhance customer satisfaction:

1. Collect and Analyze Customer Data

Types of Data:

- **Usage Data**: Track how customers use your product, including features they use most frequently, session lengths, and user paths.

- **Behavioral Data**: Analyze customer actions and interactions, such as click patterns, feature adoption rates, and engagement metrics.

- **Feedback Data**: Gather feedback through surveys, reviews, support tickets, and direct customer interactions to understand their experiences and pain points.

Tools and Techniques:

- **Analytics Platforms**: Use tools like Google Analytics, Mixpanel, or Amplitude to collect and analyze data related to user behavior and product usage.

- **Customer Feedback Tools**: Employ tools like SurveyMonkey, Qualtrics, or Zendesk to collect and analyze customer feedback.

2. Identify Key Metrics and KPIs

Important Metrics:

- **Net Promoter Score (NPS)**: Measure customer loyalty and likelihood to recommend your product. A higher NPS indicates better customer satisfaction.

- **Customer Satisfaction Score (CSAT)**: Assess overall customer satisfaction with your product or service through direct surveys.

- **Customer Effort Score (CES)**: Evaluate the ease of the customer experience by measuring how much effort customers need to resolve issues or complete tasks.

- **Churn Rate**: Monitor the percentage of customers who stop using your product over a specific period. A high churn rate indicates potential dissatisfaction.

3. Implement Data-Driven Strategies

Personalization:

- **Tailored Experiences**: Use data to personalize customer interactions and recommendations. For example, suggest features or upgrades based on their usage patterns and preferences.

- **Segmented Marketing**: Create targeted marketing campaigns and product offers based on customer segments and behavior analysis.

Proactive Support:

- **Predictive Analytics**: Utilize predictive analytics to anticipate potential issues and proactively address them before they impact customer satisfaction.

- **Automated Alerts**: Set up alerts for significant changes in customer behavior or satisfaction metrics, allowing your team to respond quickly.

Product Improvement:

- **Feature Usage Analysis**: Identify underused or problematic features and gather feedback to make data-driven improvements.

- **A/B Testing**: Conduct A/B tests to evaluate the impact of new features, changes, or updates on customer satisfaction and engagement.

4. Monitor and Adapt

Continuous Monitoring:

- **Real-Time Dashboards**: Use real-time dashboards to continuously monitor key metrics and customer feedback.

- **Regular Reviews**: Conduct regular reviews of your data and analytics to identify trends, areas for improvement, and opportunities for enhancement.

Adaptation and Iteration:

- **Responsive Changes**: Make iterative changes based on data insights and continuously refine your strategies to better meet customer needs.

- **Feedback Loop**: Create a feedback loop where data-driven insights are regularly used to inform product development, support, and marketing strategies.

Building a Community Around Your SaaS Product

Creating a strong community around your SaaS product can enhance customer engagement, loyalty, and satisfaction. A thriving community provides value to both users and the business. Here's how to build and nurture a community effectively:

1. Define Your Community Goals

Objectives:

- **Customer Engagement**: Foster engagement and interaction among users to build a sense of belonging and loyalty.

- **Knowledge Sharing**: Facilitate knowledge sharing and collaboration to help users get the most out of your product.

- **Feedback and Improvement**: Use the community as a source of feedback for product improvements and feature requests.

2. Choose the Right Platforms

Community Platforms:

- **Online Forums**: Set up online forums or discussion boards where users can ask questions, share experiences, and engage with others.

- **Social Media Groups**: Create and manage groups on social media platforms like LinkedIn, Facebook, or Twitter to connect with users and share updates.

- **Dedicated Community Sites**: Consider building a dedicated community site or portal where users can access resources, participate in discussions, and interact with the brand.

3. Foster Engagement and Interaction

Content and Activities:

- **Regular Content**: Share valuable content, such as blog posts, tutorials, case studies, and industry news, to keep the community informed and engaged.

- **Events and Webinars**: Host events, webinars, or live Q&A sessions to provide learning opportunities and facilitate real-time interaction.

- **User-Generated Content**: Encourage users to create and share their own content, such as reviews, success stories, and tips, to foster a sense of ownership and involvement.

Community Management:

- **Moderation and Support**: Ensure active moderation to maintain a positive and supportive environment. Address questions, concerns, and issues promptly.

- **Recognition and Rewards**: Recognize and reward active and valuable community members through badges, shout-outs, or exclusive access to resources.

4. Leverage Community Feedback

Feedback Collection:

- **Surveys and Polls**: Use surveys and polls to gather feedback on community activities, content, and features.

- **Discussion Threads**: Monitor discussions and threads for feedback and suggestions from community members.

Actionable Insights:

- **Incorporate Feedback**: Use community feedback to inform product development, support strategies, and content creation.

- **Transparent Communication**: Communicate openly with the community about how their feedback is being used and the impact it has on the product.

5. Build Partnerships and Collaborations

External Partnerships:

- **Influencers and Advocates**: Partner with industry influencers or brand advocates to amplify your community's reach and credibility.

- **Industry Events**: Collaborate with industry events or conferences to engage with a broader audience and build brand awareness.

Internal Collaboration:

- **Cross-Functional Teams**: Collaborate with product, marketing, and support teams to ensure alignment and support for community initiatives.

- **Customer Success Integration**: Integrate community insights with customer success efforts to enhance user experience and satisfaction.

By leveraging data and analytics to understand and enhance customer satisfaction and building a strong, engaged community around your SaaS product, you can create a more valuable and rewarding experience for your customers. This approach not only improves retention but also drives growth and strengthens your brand's position in the market.

CONCLUSION

In the ever-evolving landscape of SaaS, the journey from startup to a successful, scalable business is as challenging as it is rewarding. This book has aimed to provide a comprehensive guide to navigating the complexities of building, growing, and sustaining a B2B SaaS company. Let's recap the key takeaways and insights that will serve as a foundation for your ongoing journey.

1. Understanding B2B SaaS Dynamics

The B2B SaaS model offers distinct advantages, including recurring revenue, scalability, and deep customer relationships. Recognizing the key differences between B2B and B2C SaaS is crucial, as each requires tailored strategies to address unique customer needs and market conditions. Overcoming common myths and misconceptions about B2B SaaS can prevent costly pitfalls and guide you towards more effective practices.

2. Building a Strong Foundation

Identifying a market need and validating your idea are critical first steps. Crafting a well-thought-out business plan and vision sets a clear path for your startup, while assembling a capable founding team and securing initial funding provide the necessary resources for growth. Developing a Minimum Viable Product (MVP) helps you test your concept and gather early feedback.

3. Navigating Product Development

Understanding the product development lifecycle, choosing the right tech stack, and ensuring scalability and security are essential for creating a robust SaaS product. Prioritizing user experience and interface design, coupled with iterative development using agile methodologies, helps in delivering a product that resonates with users and adapts to changing needs.

4. Driving Market Success

Understanding your target market and customer personas, building a strong brand identity, and employing effective marketing and sales strategies are crucial for market penetration. Measuring and analyzing your efforts allows for continuous improvement and adaptation, while identifying growth opportunities and expanding your product offerings drives sustained success.

5. Scaling and Optimization

Scaling your operations and infrastructure, building a scalable customer support system, and hiring and retaining top talent are pivotal for managing growth. Implementing effective pricing models, understanding the psychology of pricing, and continuously testing and iterating your pricing strategy ensure that your pricing remains competitive and aligned with customer expectations.

6. Fostering Customer Success

Customer retention is fundamental to long-term success. Strategies for improving customer onboarding, implementing a customer success program, and using data and analytics to enhance satisfaction play vital roles in building lasting relationships.

Creating a thriving community around your SaaS product fosters engagement and loyalty, contributing to a more robust and resilient business.

Looking Forward

The SaaS industry is dynamic, with new challenges and opportunities emerging regularly. Staying informed about industry trends, continuously refining your strategies, and adapting to evolving customer needs will keep your business competitive and successful. Embrace innovation, listen to your customers, and remain agile to navigate the future of SaaS with confidence.

As you embark on or continue your journey in the B2B SaaS space, remember that success is a continuous process of learning, adapting, and growing. This book has provided a roadmap, but your unique insights, dedication, and perseverance will ultimately shape your path. May your SaaS venture thrive and make a lasting impact in the world of technology and beyond.

Thank you for joining me on this journey, and best of luck with your SaaS endeavors.